# Cani Corsi

Katie Gillespie

www.openlightbox.com

**Step 1**
Go to **www.openlightbox.com**

**Step 2**
Enter this unique code

**VAHEGWC10**

**Step 3**
Explore your interactive eBook!

**AV2 is optimized for use on any device**

# Your interactive eBook comes with...

**Contents**
Browse a live contents page to easily navigate through resources

**Audio**
Listen to sections of the book read aloud

**Videos**
Watch informative video clips

**Weblinks**
Gain additional information for research

**Slideshows**
View images and captions

**Try This!**
Complete activities and hands-on experiments

**Key Words**
Study vocabulary, and complete a matching word activity

**Quizzes**
Test your knowledge

**Share**
Share titles within your Learning Management System (LMS) or Library Circulation System

**Citation**
Create bibliographical references following the Chicago Manual of Style

**This title is part of our AV2 digital subscription**

**1-Year K–5 Subscription**
**ISBN** 978-1-7911-3320-7

Access hundreds of AV2 titles with our digital subscription.
Sign up for a FREE trial at **www.openlightbox.com/trial**

# Cani Corsi

## Contents

# Name That Dog

Which dog is originally from Italy?

Which dog is confident and strong-willed?

Which dog comes in many colors?

Which dog loves to be with its family?

Did you guess the Cane Corso?

You are right!

# An Ancient Breed

The Cane Corso **breed** has a long and rich history. A group of ancient Greeks called the Molossians are thought to have bred large working dogs. These giant animals, known as Molossers, may have played a role in the origins of the Cane Corso.

When armies from **ancient Rome** invaded Greece, they brought some Molossers back to Italy. It is believed that these dogs were crossed with Italian breeds. Over time, this led to today's Cani Corsi, as the dogs are known in groups.

Italy is a European country that extends into the Mediterranean Sea. It shares its western border with France, northern border with Switzerland and Austria, and eastern border with Slovenia.
Switzerland
Austria
Hungary
Slovenia
France
Italy
Croatia
Bosnia and Herzegovina
Mediterranean Sea

For hundreds of years, Corsi were common in the southern Italian countryside. However, their population fell during the two **world wars** in the first half of the 20th century. After the world wars, there were so few Corsi left that they almost became **extinct**. Fortunately, in the 1970s, fans of the breed came together to save it. Their efforts helped the breed's numbers recover.

With the Corso's numbers on the rise, the breed began to spread outside of Italy. The first **litter** of Corsi came to live in the United States in 1988. They were imported from Italy by a dog breeder named Michael Sottile. However, the American Kennel Club (AKC) did not recognize the breed until 2010.

The AKC is an organization that groups dog breeds together. The dogs in each category all share certain traits. There are seven different AKC categories. Corsi belong to the Working Group, along with breeds such as the Portuguese water dog, Siberian husky, and Newfoundland. As the group's name suggests, these animals often have jobs. Some of their skills may include sled pulling or water rescues.

A Corso can weigh more than 100 pounds (45 kilograms).

# What Corsi Look Like

Corsi are medium to large dogs. Adult females stand between 23.5 and 26 inches (60 and 66 centimeters) high. Adult males are a bit larger, ranging from 25 to 27.5 inches (63.5 to 70 cm) high.

These sturdy dogs are known for being muscular and strong. They have athletic, well-balanced bodies with large bones. A Corso's front feet are round, with arched toes like those of a cat. The dog's back feet are more oval-shaped.

Corsi have stiff, shiny **coats**. The hairs are short and coarse, making the coats waterproof. Below their dense fur, a Corso has a light undercoat. In cold winter weather, it grows thicker to help the animal keep warm.

A Corso's fur can come in many different colors. These include black, red, and several shades of gray or **fawn**. All of these colors may be brindled. This means that they are brown or a sandy color called tawny, with streaks or spots of other colors.

Corsi have triangle-shaped ears. Sometimes, owners decide to have them **cropped**. When this happens, the outer ear flap is removed. Other owners leave their Corso's ears natural.

A Corso's muzzle takes up about one third of the length of the dog's head.

# The Corso Personality

The Corso is often described as a majestic dog. This breed is confident and can be quite headstrong. Corsi are also intelligent, with a good attention span. This makes them particularly good working dogs that are easily trainable.

Corsi are extremely loyal to their families and will protect them. Combined with their large size and power, this trait may make Corsi appear threatening to outsiders. However, it is also why Corsi are so renowned as guard dogs.

Corsi respond well to positive training. Punishments should not be used when training these dogs.

Due to their strong-willed nature, Corsi are recommended for experienced dog owners.

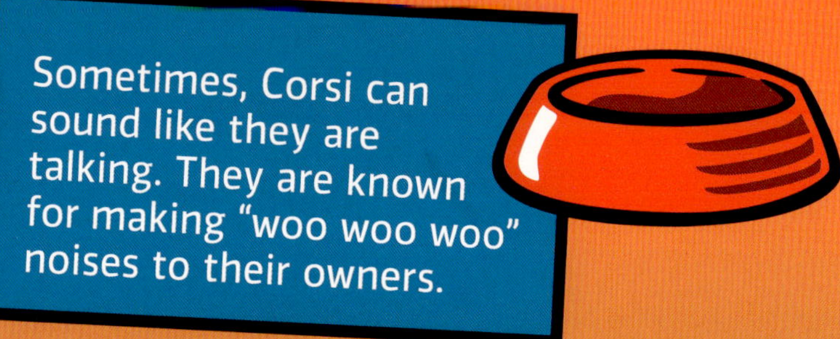


Although they have many positive qualities, Corsi are not the right fit for everybody. Corso owners need to match their dog's dominant nature and lead the **pack**. It is also important that all family members are up to owning this breed. Corsi do not belong in a home with people who are afraid of large dogs.

Despite their tough outward appearance, Corsi are actually very sensitive. They have high social needs and get very attached to their people. Corsi are known to have **separation anxiety**. Training can help ensure that the dogs will behave when left alone.

# Corso Puppies

As a general rule, big dog breeds tend to have more puppies in their litters than small breeds. Given the dog's size, a Corso's litter usually ranges from about 6 to 10 puppies.

Large breeds often take longer to reach maturity than small breeds. However, not all puppies grow at the same rate. Many Cani Corsi will finish growing at 19 months of age. Others do not reach their full adult size until they are two years old.

Spending short amounts of time alone in a well-fenced yard can help with a young Corso's training. This can help the dog grow more confident on its own and teach it that its owner will always return home.

Experts recommend **socialization** for all dog breeds. However, this is especially important for big, strong dogs such as Corsi. Their protective and dominant traits mean that socialization should be done as early as possible, starting when they are puppies.

Corso owners must also be willing to train their new puppies. It is crucial for the dogs to understand that their owner is the boss. This will help Corsi become obedient and well behaved as they get older. Fortunately, Corsi are eager to please, which makes training them easier than many other breeds.

Staying calm, confident, and consistent during training can help a Corso know who is in charge.

The history of ancient Roman dog breeds has been documented through statues and paintings.

# Corsi Hard at Work

The Corso's early ancestors were war dogs for the ancient Romans. Their ferocity and size made them very intimidating. During battle, these dogs would charge enemy lines while carrying buckets of flaming oil.

After ancient Roman civilization fell, these devoted dogs continued to work in other jobs. Many were used to hunt wild boar. They also worked on farms where they drove cattle, pulled carts, and helped guard the property and livestock.

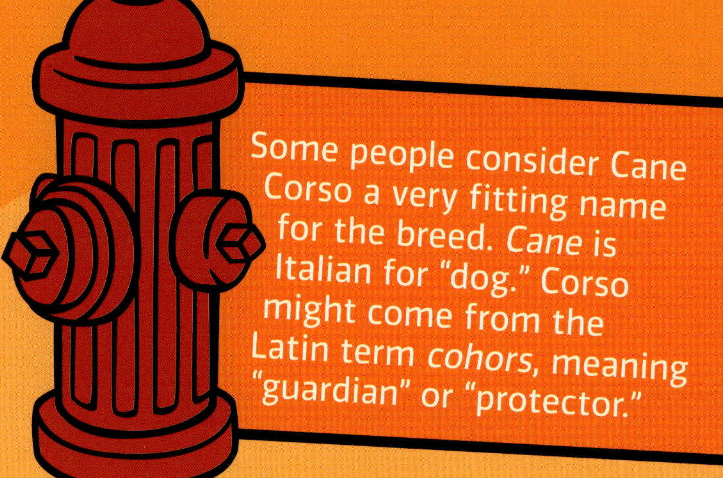


Today, the Corso remains one of the best watchdog breeds. Some dogs work in stores, providing protection or even greeting customers. Corsi can still be found on farms as well, serving as animal herders and guard dogs.

Many Corsi now compete in dog shows and sports. They are particularly talented in events that involve tracking, obedience, or agility. These kinds of activities provide good mental and physical exercise. This is important for all dogs, but especially for large, smart breeds, such as Corsi.

Corsi enjoy having work to do and need to be kept busy. A bored Corso may bark or dig up yards.

Young Corsi should be taken for short, slow walks. This helps their bodies develop properly over their first 18 months to two years.

# Caring for a Cane Corso

Since Corsi **shed**, they need to be brushed regularly. Once a week is enough for most of the year. During the spring shedding season, Corsi should be brushed every day.

Like other dogs, Corsi must have their ears checked and cleaned regularly. They also need to have their teeth brushed using a special dog toothpaste. Nails should be trimmed every two to four weeks. Baths can be given as necessary.

While Corsi need plenty of time outside, they should not be left alone in the yard for too long. Outdoor exercise with their families will make them the happiest. Corsi love to come along on hikes, runs, or bike rides.

A 2017 survey found that coat color may relate to a Corso's life span. Of all the dogs that participated, those with black brindle coats lived the longest.

Adult Corsi should be taken for at least a 1-mile (1.6-kilometer) walk twice a day, once in the morning and once in the evening. They also need 20 minutes of playing, working, or training time each day.

Owning a dog is a lifelong commitment. It can be hard work, but also very rewarding. Corsi have a life span of about 10 to 12 years. They are typically healthy dogs. However, Corsi may suffer from certain conditions. These include eyelid problems, **epilepsy**, and hip issues. Breeders should have the heart, hips, and elbows of their puppies tested while they are young.

Due to their size, Corsi are at high risk of a health problem called bloat. To help avoid it, dogs should be fed twice a day instead of being given one large meal. They should be encouraged to eat slowly as well.

# Cane Corso Quiz

**Q: How much can Corsi weigh?**

A: More than 100 pounds (45 kg)

**Q: Which jobs did Corsi often do on farms?**

A: Driving cattle, pulling carts, and guarding property and livestock

**Q: When did the first litter of Corsi come to the United States?**

A: 1988

**Q: At what age do many Corsi finish growing?**

A: 19 months

**Q: How often should a Corso's nails be trimmed?**

A: Every two to four weeks

**Q: What does the Italian word *Cane* mean in English?**

A: Dog

# Key Words

**ancient Rome** (AYN-chnt ROHM): a civilization centered around the Italian city of Rome that began in about 750 BC and lasted until 476 AD

**breed** (BREED): a certain type of animal

**coats** (KOHTS): the fur of dogs

**cropped** (KRAWPT): cut a piece off the ear of an animal

**epilepsy** (EH-puh-lep-see): a disease that can cause seizures

**extinct** (ukh-STINGKT): no longer existing on Earth

**fawn** (FAWN): a light yellowish brown color

**litter** (LI-tr): a group of babies born to one animal at the same time

**pack** (PAK): a group of animals that live together

**separation anxiety** (seh-puh-RAY-shn ang-ZAI-uh-tee): when a dog becomes extremely stressed while its owners are away

**shed** (SHED): when fur naturally falls off

**socialization** (so-shuh-lai-ZAY-shn): helping puppies become comfortable around people and other animals in different environments

**world wars** (WURLD WORZ): two wars involving all the major countries of the world; World War I lasted from 1914 to 1918 and World War II lasted from 1939 to 1945

# Index

# Get the best of both worlds.

AV2 bridges the gap between print and digital.

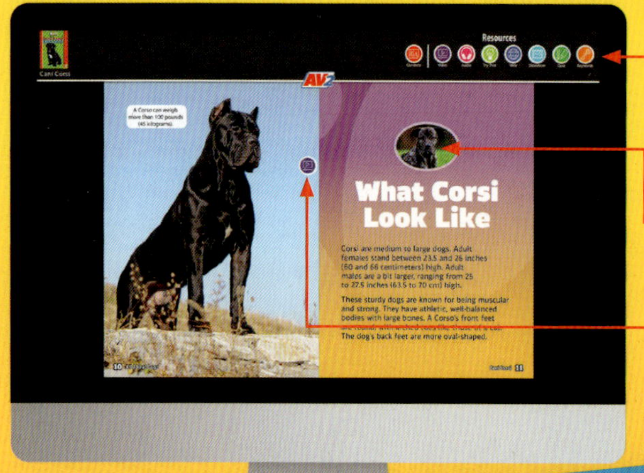


The expandable resources toolbar enables quick access to content including **videos**, **audio**, **activities**, **weblinks**, **slideshows**, **quizzes**, and **key words**.

**Animated videos** make static images come alive.

Resource icons on each page help readers to further **explore key concepts**.


Published by Lightbox Learning Inc.
276 5th Avenue, Suite 704 #917
New York, NY 10001
Website: www.openlightbox.com





Library of Congress Control Number: 2022933071

ISBN 978-1-7911-4803-4 (hardcover)
ISBN 978-1-7911-4804-1 (softcover)
ISBN 978-1-7911-4328-2 (multi-user eBook)

Printed in Guangzhou, China
1 2 3 4 5 6 7 8 9 0 26 25 24 23 22

022022
101321

Project Coordinator: John Willis
Designer: Terry Paulhus

Photo Credits
Every reasonable effort has been made to trace ownership and to obtain permission to reprint copyright material. The publisher would be pleased to have any errors or omissions brought to its attention so that they may be corrected in subsequent printings. The publisher acknowledges Alamy, Getty Images, Shutterstock, and Wikimedia as its primary image suppliers for this title.